So
You Want
To Write

So You Want To Write

A Step-By-Step Plan
To Help You Write Your Book

Joanne Putnam

The Ready Scribe
Plymouth, Wisconsin

So You Want To Write
A Step-By-Step Plan to Help You Write Your Book
Revised Edition

By Joanne Putnam

Published by:

    The Ready Scribe
    C/O Joanne Putnam
    Plymouth, WI 53073 U.S.A.

Library of Congress Cataloging-in-Publication Data

Putnam, Joanne
  So You Want To Write: A Step-By-Step Plan for Writing Your Book
  ISBN 0-9705098-1-2
    1. Authorship

808.02

Table of Contents

Introduction

"How do you get started writing?" "How do you get published?" "How do you write a book?" I have heard these questions asked over and over. Are they questions you have asked? Is there a book inside you?

You have probably had the idea for ages and talked about it for years. You feel the Lord compelling you to write. People are entreating you to write. The title mulls over and over in your mind and perhaps you've written a couple of chapters. But how do you get everything down in print?

The answers to these questions are contained in this book. *So You Want To Write* will motivate you to finally get started writing. It will give you tools and resources to help you write well. And it will direct and encourage you to go all the way to the finished project!

I don't claim to be an expert on writing. I just know that when you feel God is prompting you to do something, you need to know how to go about doing it. God is urging people to write, but they hold back because they don't know where to begin and they are afraid to fail. This book is an attempt to give them the encouragement and resources they need to fulfill the work God has called them to.

It's wonderful to have the encouragement of others, however, unless you put pen to paper or fingers to the keyboard, it will not get written. You have a message that only you can share. You have a life to change. You have a job to do. Do not delay!

Acknowledgements

I want to thank Jesus for His help in writing this book. Several times I put it aside, thinking I would wait until I had more time to work on it, only to be reminded by the Lord that there was a need for such a resource.

I want to thank all the wonderful people who responded to my survey. Writers are busy people and I was honored to think that over half of those I contacted, took time to respond. Their valuable advice is spread throughout the pages of this book. I so appreciate the following respondents: Gayla Baughman, Crawford D. Coon, Cindy Chubboy, Carol Clemans, Marvelle Dees, Lynda Allison Doty, Shirley Englehardt, Roffie Ensey, Nona Freeman, Valda Johnson, LaJoyce Martin, Arlo Moehlenpall, Nan Pamer, J.T. Pugh, David M. Reeves, Kenneth V. Reeves, Ruth Rieder, David Sanzo, Daniel L. Segraves, Judy Segraves, Jim H. Yohe, and Thomas Weisser.

I want to thank Margie McNall, from the Pentecostal Publishing House, who has been so encouraging, helpful and patient with me.

Special thanks goes to those who did editing for me: Darlene Becker, Krista Knudson, and my daughter Amy Grinnell. They weren't afraid to tear it up and help me put it back together, and they saved me a lot of embarrassment!

I also want to thank my husband, Rev. John Putnam, for his daily encouragement. He has been the greatest blessing to my life. I love him dearly.

Chapter 1

Don't Die With the Book Inside You

Would you like to share ideas, thoughts and insight that you have gleaned through the years? Would you like to offer something for people to take home with them to help them study and grow spiritually? Would you like to provide a resource that reaches beyond your personal ability to touch people's lives? If you can answer any of these questions with an affirmative, "yes," then **you** should write a book!

I have no doubt that for years you've been saying, "I ought to write a book!" Perhaps it has always been a dream of yours to write, or the Lord has recently quickened your heart and mind to write. It could be that others have been requesting you to write so they can have a tangible reference or source of information you have shared in your teaching or ministry. Maybe they feel a copy of your testimony or life story would be an encouragement and witness to others. There may be a friend or loved one whose story you have always felt should be in print and you have considered writing about them. So why aren't you writing?

All of us have a story to tell, but we don't feel qualified to tell it or we don't know where to begin. This book will guide you in the process of compiling, writing and publishing your book. It will provide the tools you need to hone your craft. If you will follow the step by step guidelines in this book, you will have the material needed to publish your book.

Writing a book is not an overnight process. It takes self-discipline and commitment. You don't need to quit your job to do it, but you will need to make time within your daily routine to spend time with pen in hand or hands on the keyboard! You will need to set realistic goals and timelines. And you will need to germinate "thick skin" if you don't already have it!

I really believe that what keeps most people from writing is the **fear of failure**. We all took the required English classes and wrote the necessary papers. And we all had papers returned dripping with the blood of the red editing pen! Let's face it. It's hard to get past those memories!

I didn't think I was that bad of a writer until my third quarter freshman English class at The University of Akron. Our Professor had warned us that he was the department chair and **the** best English Professor we would ever have. At the end of the sixth week of the ten week quarter, our first papers were returned. His comments have been forever etched in my mind: **"F- I did not want a handy dandy little summary of what drama is..."**

I couldn't believe it! I had never had an F- on anything! What else did he want when he asked the question: "What is Drama?" It didn't even console me that over two-thirds of the class had received the same grade! How could I ever write a book with this in my background? The answer: Thick skin!

I realized that what Jesus had given me to share was worth taking the risks and spending the time necessary to birth my first book *A Time To Grow...* From that first bold step, I went on to write magazine articles, editorials, newsletters and my most recent book, *Growing in All the Right Places*.

Irving Benig, author of *The Messiah Stones*, said of his first book, "My real crisis of confidence was the initial question: Could I do it? Before you worry about getting an agent, before you worry about whether a book is good or not, the real test is, can you do it? Can you finish it? But once I started writing it, I got more and more confident."

Florence Littauer, one of my favorite writers, in her book *Silver Boxes*, shares a story about her father. When she was a senior in college she went home for Christmas break to visit with her parents and her two brothers. She had a couple of quiet moments with her father and he led her to a little den in the back of the store where they lived. He pulled a cigar box out from behind their old upright piano and opened it to show her a little pile of newspaper articles. She asked what they were, and he explained to her that they were articles he had written and some letters to the editor that had been published.

She questioned her father, "Why didn't you tell me you could write?" She was a senior in college, studying creative writing, and she had no idea her father had produced articles good enough for publication.

"Why didn't you tell me you'd done this?" she asked again.

"Because I didn't want your mother to know," he responded. "She's always told me that since I didn't have much education I shouldn't try to write. When each item would be printed, I'd cut it out and hide it in this box. I knew someday I'd show the box to someone, and it's you."

He told Florence that he had recently submitted an article to his denomination's ministerial magazine and was awaiting its publication. As she examined the contents of the box, she found various items, including a detailed personal letter from a prominent senator who had written a thankful response commenting on how insightful her father's suggestions had been in an article he had written.

The day after he shared this precious box with Florence, he was tragically killed. Forever dashed were his aspirations of becoming a writer.

How about you? Should you write a book? Only you know the answer to that question. Ask God to direct you in His perfect will. Ask Him to complete in you the perfect work He has set out to do. If you still feel His leading to write, ask Him to help you by giving you wisdom and direction in the writing process and production of your book. Be willing to take the risks and time needed to birth the work that the Lord has placed upon you to do. If Jesus is truly leading you to do a work for Him, He will help you to accomplish it.

Oliver Wendell Holmes once said, "Many of us die with the music still in us." I say, "Don't die with the book still inside you!"

Chapter 2

So Where Do I Begin?

You are probably working on a manuscript right now or you would not have purchased this book. Before you go any further, I would suggest that you read completely through *So You Want To Write* to gain helpful insight into the process of writing and self-publishing. Writing and getting published can be an arduous adventure. I've learned that the more I study and research at the beginning of a project, the less stress I have as I progress through it. Researching the nuts and bolts of the process will ultimately save you time, energy and money.

One of the first things you need to do is decide what kind of book you will write. Will it be fiction (children's books, westerns, mysteries) or nonfiction (biography, autobiography, devotional, history, Bible study guide, on doctrine, a witnessing tool about salvation, prayer, life principles, or on relationships)? Is it poetry?

Also you must decide why you will write and who your audience will be. Will you write to inform, teach or inspire? Who will read your book? Knowing your potential audience will help you to focus your writing to best meet their needs. Whatever genre you choose to write in, you need to keep your audience in mind and your book's sales potential if you plan to at least break even with your costs.

Poetry and fiction are very difficult to sell, and according to research, have a short sales life. They are no less anointed, but people who buy books are often looking for something to help them grow spiritually in their Christian walk and nonfiction books tend to meet those needs better.

Dan Poynter (*Is There A Book Inside You*) says "A lot of fiction is written each year but comparatively little is published." He says for fiction to be successful the writer needs to carefully consider his audience first and write specifically for them. Poynter states that "Because fiction is entertainment, the writer must be extremely creative and be able to tell a story well." If you write well and produce good fiction, you will develop a "following" and people will begin to look specifically for your books. La Joyce Martin, Janet Oke, and Beverly Lewis are examples of Christian fiction writers that have a tremendous "following." Their fans cannot wait until the next book comes out!

I recently shared a book table with a wonderful person who had self-published a lovely book of poetry with hand-drawn illustrations. It was geared to a specific holiday that was approaching and it was "hot off the press." The new author was confident the books would sell out in the few days of the conference. Beautiful handmade gift cards were available to provide the perfect holiday gift for that certain someone. I watched the disappointment grow in the young author's eyes as the conference wore on and very few sales were made. In an effort to recoup some of her expenses, she changed her sign over and over until the books and cards were nearly half price. I wish someone had warned this zealous author about the track record of poetry. The seasonal nature of her book further limited her sales. Many poets self-publish simply to share with loved ones and friends, but unfortunately, few actually find profit in the venue.

Nonfiction is actually much easier to write and sell. The content is often what people are looking for and if people know you by name and respect what you have to say, they will purchase your book. Nonfiction books usually have a particular purpose, which may be to inform (biography, autobiography, history), to teach (how to pray, study the Bible, learn to relate to people, be a better spouse), to persuade (witnessing, doctrine), or to inspire (devotional, encouragement to overcome difficult situations, or something just to lift your spirits and make you laugh). A nonfiction book with a good idea that is fresh and sharply focused, will sell.

You need to decide if your idea is big enough to fill an entire book. To be considered a book according to international standards, it must have at least 50 pages. Booklets are more cost effective to produce and they sell well. Sometimes they are purchased in bulk to be used as give-aways by churches, organizations, or businesses. Some topics are very 'timely' issues and producing them in booklet form would make them available sooner. Keep in mind that booklets contain specific information on a specific topic. Perhaps you have several different topics that you have considered lumping together in one book that might be better presented in separate booklets.

Writing a book in your field is an enriching learning experience. It will make you better at what you do by forcing you to research and study. The process of organizing, condensing and classifying information, clarifies the data in your own mind and serves to sharpen your own understanding of the topic as you share it with the reader.

In deciding on a topic to write about, the key phrase is "find a need and fill it!" *So You Want To Write*, grew out of people continually asking questions about writing. They asked about Christian writing classes, book printers, publishers, editing and all sorts of other questions. I have always encouraged people to write, and I have shared as much as I could in the limited time available. But I've always thought how nice it would be to have something tangible for them to take with them that would be practical, down to earth, and useful, a resource that could answer specific questions and helps people through the process. This particular book grew from the perceived need of others who were interested in writing. It contains information gleaned from my own research and personal experience that I am endeavoring to share with those who desire such information.

It is obvious from the survey I sent to over fifty self-published authors, that few Christian writers read secular books on how to write or how to self-publish. Perhaps writers don't know they are available, or they don't believe that they would answer their questions or meet their particular needs. Again, when you know you can trust the author, you feel comfortable listening to their advice, so that's why I'm sharing!

What are **you** supposed to share? What principles of life has God entrusted to your understanding that you need to impart to others? Are people asking for a copy of your notes after you speak? This is a clear indication that there is a need for you to write!

Hopefully by now, you know what you are going to write, be it fiction or nonfiction. The next chapter will help you to decide the best way to go about publishing your material and how to publish it in the most cost effective manner.

Chapter 3

How Do I Get In Print?

Now you need to decide how you will publish your work. How will you place what you have written before the public? There are actually several options and I would like for you to carefully consider each one.

Conventional Publishing

Traditionally, books were published by large publishing houses in New York or Chicago. After the book is written, the author looks for an agent to peddle it to the large Christian houses or queries the publishing company on their own. Some of the well-known Christian publishing houses are: Zondervan, Tyndale, Focus on the Family, Eerdmans, Bethany House, Baker Books, Harvest House, Multnomah, Cook Communications, Moody Press, Standard Publishing and more.

The process of querying various publishing houses, in search of a sale, is very time consuming. Even after a sale, there is generally a wait of eighteen to twenty-four months before the book actually reaches the shelves.

Once a book is purchased by a traditional publisher, the author has no say on the book's final title, how it will be presented on the cover, or what changes will be made in the text. The author may be asked for input, but the final decision is up to the editing staff of the publisher

Keep in mind that publishers print books in order to make money. Large publishers care little about the content or the wishes of the author. They do not want to run the risk of financial loss so they "market" the book as a commodity.

As the author, **if** a conventional publisher picks up your book, you can expect to receive 10-15% of the sales price in royalties. If for any reason they discount your book, you will probably not receive anything on the sales of the discounted books.

The publishing industry has changed dramatically in the past few years. Publishers take the risk with each book they publish as to whether it will sell or not. They are more reluctant than ever to publish a book from a first time author. They want to publish authors who already have a selling track record or publish books written by "big names" who have their own following and are all but guaranteed to sell. Out of the 350,000 manuscripts that are submitted to traditional publishers each year, 32.000 go to print. Large publishing companies receive between 15,000 and 20,000 unsolicited manuscripts each year. Simon & Schuster say they publish less than 1% of all the unsolicited manuscripts they receive.

Publishers have found that even after selecting the best manuscripts they can find, and promoting them, three in ten will sell well, four in ten will break even and three will be losers. Statistics show large companies must sell close to 10,000 copies of a book just to break even.

All of this makes it tougher than ever to get a book published through traditional means, so more and more people are choosing to self-publish.

Specialized Publishers

Today there are many smaller, specialized publishers that print books designed to meet the needs of their constituents: Word Aflame Press, Gospel Publishing House, St. Mary's Press, Charisma House, Chosen Books and hundreds of other companies publish Christian books.

With these publishers, an agent needed is rarely needed. They publish well-established authors on topics that they know will sell. They hesitate to publish a book from a first time author unless it is a subject they feel meets their current need. If this is the way you would like to go, you need to query them (send them a detailed letter letting them know what you are writing and try to interest them in publishing your book). There are many books available to help you in this process. The appendix of this book has a list of books you may want to read. Most are probably available through your local library system.

Sally Stuart publishes the *Christian Writer's Market Guide* every year. It lists hundreds of Christian publishers and publications, gives details as to what types of manuscripts individual publishers are looking for, and gives specific names and addresses as to who to contact at each company. The *Christian Writer's Market Guide* also lists compete information about magazines and newsletters that may be interested in publishing nonfiction and fiction articles you have written. It lists hundreds of resources for writers, book publishers, subsidy publishers, gives market analysis telling what is currently selling, tells of writing contests and conferences, gives information about writing groups, editorial services, literary agents and plenty of valuable information to help you hone in on hot topics. The *Christian Writer's Market Guide* is published yearly and can be ordered from the author, through a local bookstore or online. (See *Resources* in the back of this book.)

Royalties from specialized publishers are the same as conventional publishers. The author receives an average of 10-15% royalty on the sale of each book. He or she can usually purchase books at a discount to sell on their own. Again, books that are discounted rarely pay a royalty though the author may have the option of buying remaining stock from the publisher and market it on his or her own.

Subsidy Publishing

The third option for publishing is what is candidly referred to as "Vanity Presses." Which are just that. They publish anyone's work for payment whether it is worthy of publishing or not! Watch out for these scams! Most people who write have very sensitive feelings and there are people and groups who will take advantage of their naivete.

Vanity presses are often listed in the Yellow Pages under "Publishers." You see their advertisements in various magazines. Recent ads I've read include these statements: Authors Wanted, Make it Happen, Your Dreams Can Come True, Books in 10 days or less, Writers Wanted, Publish Your Book At A Price You Can Afford, Award Winning Professional Publishing Services, and various other catchy headlines.

Vanity presses accept almost everything they receive and do so with glowing reviews. No rejects here! They make no promises regarding sales and statistics show the book usually sells fewer than 100 copies! The vanity publisher doesn't have to sell any books because the author has already paid for the work. The subsidy publisher only wants to manufacture the book, not edit, promote, sell or distribute it.

Editors say when they receive copies of subsidy published books for review, they usually just throw them in the trashcan. Reviewers are leery of them because they know little attention is paid to editing. One author said that having the name of a vanity publisher on the spine of the book is "a kiss of death."

The company promises to promote your book in well read periodicals but in actuality it receives very little individual attention. Reportedly, they purchase ad space in large newspapers and simply print a list of titles available through their company with no information as to what the book is about. This type of advertising does not sell books.

The author pays for all printing at inflated prices and rarely sees a return for his or her money. Statistics show that the author actually pays more than the printing bill, usually between $10,000 and $30,000 and receives only 40% of the retail price when the books are sold. There have been several lawsuits involving these types of organizations. Very few people seem to be satisfied having taken this route. I have heard of situations where people paid thousands of dollars and received only a few copies of the book with the promise that the remainder was warehoused at their company, only to find out the few books they received were all that were actually printed! "Beware!" say Attorney Generals in the many states that are and have taken these institutions to court.

If you are a poet, you need to be aware of poetry contests. A former student of mine recently showed me her "winning entry" from a poetry contest she had entered. The "prize" consisted of being printed in a volume of "winning" poetry submissions that cost the poet $49.95 to purchase, plus shipping and handling! Usually the author must pay a submission fee of $25.00 or more just to enter the contest, so I doubt that many entries are not winners! And at the exorbitant price of the book, it is not going to be a best seller at Barnes and Nobles!

E-books

E-books are the new revolution in the publishing industry. E-books are books that are downloaded from the Internet onto electronic tablets, cell phones and other devices. They can easily access any books that are available for downloading.

They are cheap to produce because everything is done electronically and are accessible to anyone who has the Internet. E-books can be purchased or borrowed for a limited time.

E-books go hand in hand with Print on Demand (POD) books.

Print on demand

Print on demand is a recent concept that goes along with the next option I will present, People who choose to self-publish can opt to have books available only online as a download, or printed, as they need them, "on demand." Books are printed as they are sold. This reduces the number of books that are initially printed, eliminates the extra cost of reprint set-up charges and reduces the need for storage. Print on demand has been around long enough that there are several reputable companies available to work with. To name just a few: Kindle Direct Publishing, Lulu, Leanpub, Lightning Source, Xilibris, Blurb, Xulon and many others.

Self-publishing

Self-publishing is the avenue that many writers are pursuing today, and for various reasons.

Some people self-publish to save the amount of time it takes their book to get in print. Self-publishing can get your book to market two to four months after your manuscript is completed. A considerable time saving compared to traditional publishers.

Others self-publish to remain in complete control of the manuscript's content. As I mentioned earlier, traditional publishers have the right to change every aspect of your material once you have signed your rights over to them for an agreed upon fee or royalty.

Some writers choose to self-publish purely for financial reasons. Standard publishers finance the project but they only offer a royalty on sales, the norm being around 10%. If your book is chosen to be in a book club or discounted in any way, you may not receive any royalties at all. When you finance the publication of your own book, depending on the price of the book and the cost to print it, you can make as much as 75% or more profit.

Another reason to self-publish is so your book can remain in print for a longer period of time. My first book was marketed aggressively by the publisher for the typical one year. After that, sales fell and eventually they were clearanced. If you self-publish you are able to continue to pursue sales avenues and your book can remain on the market longer. As time goes on you can update your book with current information, reprint it, and continue to sell it.

A Word of Caution

As you can see, there are many options to consider in publishing your book. I would caution you to think through each alternative carefully and talk with people who have tried the various avenues before you make your decision.

Whatever you decide to do, it will entail a contract of some sort. It is very important to read everything with extreme care. If there is anything you don't understand, seek the advice of a lawyer. New writers are so excited to finally be published that they sign on the dotted line without knowing the rights they are signing off on. Tom and Marilyn Ross in *The Complete Guide to Self-Publishing*, give specific information to look for in a contract with a traditional publisher and they share specific information they have received from qualified professionals.

I have chosen to self-publish, as have hundreds of authors, but self-publishing is not for everyone. Before you choose to self-publish there are many things you should consider. The next chapter is devoted to the entire process of self-publishing. It is intended to help you decide if it is an option that you should pursue.

Chapter 4

Why Self-Publish?

Self-publishing is not a new concept. Ben Franklin was the first to self-publish. Mark Twain originally self-published *Huckleberry Finn*. Zane Grey's first novel was rejected by several publishers so he self-published. The infamous *Robert's Rules of Order* and one of the best books to aid your writing, *The Elements of Style*, by William Strunk Jr. and E. B. White were also self-published. Rod Mc Kuen's book of poetry, *Listen To The Warm*, sold 40,000 copies before Random House picked it up. *Feed Me – I'm Yours*, was rejected by 49 publishers before she decided to self-publish. She sold 300,000 copies of her self-published version, then sold rights to Bantam who went on to distribute eight million more copies.More recently, *The Christmas Box*, written by Richard Paul Evans has sold more than 7 million copies, and Evan's, *Who Moved My Cheese* is currently on the New York Times Best Sellers List. The list goes on and on with names such as: Upton Sinclair, Carl Sandburg, James Joyce, Ezra Pound, Stephen Crane, George Bernard Shaw, Edgar Allen Poe, Rudyard Kipling, Henry David Thoreau, and Walt Whitman.

Unfortunately many publishers today are not interested in whether a book is good, they are only interested in whether they think it will sell. Oftentimes they do not pick up a book until it has become a best seller from a self-publisher. There have been many best sellers that were originally and still continue to be self-published. *What Color Is Your Parachute*, written by a minister who approached several traditional publishers but to no avail, was on the NY Times Bestseller's List for 288 weeks and has sold over 5 million copies. He has since had many offers by big name companies, to purchase the rights to his book, but after 22 editions he continues to self-publish. Rather than compete with the 350,000 book-length manuscripts that are submitted to publishing houses each year, many authors are choosing to self-publish.

Rejection

Rejection is what has propelled the self-publishing industry. Good writers are tired of being told that their writing is unacceptable!

I have heard of writers who received so many rejection slips they literally wallpapered a bathroom with them!

Rejection is just a given when you submit your work to magazines and book publishers. One writing teacher challenged his class to see how many rejection slips the students could acquire during the timeframe of the class he was teaching. He did this not to see how poorly his students could write, but rather to encourage them to actually send their writing out. One student noted that he received thirty-six rejection notices and then he sold an article! That one acceptance erased the pain of the thirty-six rejections!

Because the traditional publishing industry has gone through some major changes in the past few years, they take on fewer risks. They are not willing to take on a project unless they know it is a moneymaker. Self-publishing has actually helped them to minimize their risks. If they see a self-published book that is doing well, they are eager to pick it up. Or they may be more willing to publish the next book the author writes. Sometimes they loose in the end because the author may enjoy the greater profit margin and decide he wants to continue to self-publish.

"The old school" looked down their noses at self-publishers, telling them that evidently their writing wasn't good enough to really be published, but that tide has overwhelmingly changed over the past twenty-five years.

The infamous *Chicken Soup For The Soul* series was rejected by over 150 publishers before a small health organization chose to publish it. Proof that publishers aren't always able to spot the potential best sellers!

Sales

Self-published books sell well too. I already mentioned figures for *What Color Is Your* Parachute, and *The Christmas Box*, but there are many more that have sold millions. *The One Minute* Manager has sold 12,000,000 copies and has been printed in 25 different languages. *Fifty Simple Things You Can Do to Save the Earth* has sold over 3.5 million copies. *Feed Me I'm Yours,* and *How To Keep Your Volkswagen Alive* have each sold over 2.2 million copies. And *Leadership Secrets of Attila the Hun* has sold over 500,000. Surely your book will be more interesting than that title!

As I prepared to write this book, I surveyed over fifty authors that have self-published in order to gain their insight and expertise in the process of self-publishing as well as writing in general. Throughout the book you will see their answers to various questions. Self-publishing is certainly a viable consideration, and sharing this option in depth, is one purpose of writing this book.

Why You Should Self-Publish

Self-publishing allows the author to bypass all the middlemen. The author deals directly with the printer and then handles the marketing and sales. He or she maintains complete control over the book. The self-publisher invests time as well as money, but the rewards are far greater.

Self-publishing has its risks and its rewards. You do the writing, the editing, the typesetting, and you contract with the printer. You choose the artwork, you store the books, market them, and pay for everything. It is a lot of work and a lot of risk! As a self-publisher, you have the responsibility normally relegated to many people. But, if you do it right, you will find it well worth the effort!

Your reward is that you will have produced a product that ministers to people and helps them to grow in their relationship with the Lord Jesus Christ! If you do most of the work yourself, there is also a financial reward far greater than you would receive had you gone the traditional way of publishing. Depending on the costs to produce the book, you will probably receive between 60% to 75% profit opposed to the average of 10% with conventional publishing.

When you self-publish, you write as you feel led, without the fear of an editor changing your thoughts and ideas. You determine the title, knowing it will not be changed, and you design the cover how you want it to be. And, guess what: if there are typos you get the blame!

As a self-publisher you have all the responsibility to get your book literally from your brain to the printed, bound page. You are not only the writer, you are the editor, designer/artist, typesetter, printing contractor, financier, promotions director, warehouser, shipping department, legal adviser and business manager. You can do as little or as much of the work in producing your book as you would like to but keep in mind, the more work you farm out, the less your overall profit will be.

Self-publishing takes a huge commitment of time, to be successful. Not only in the actual writing, but in the revision/editing, production and promotion stages. You must be organized and focused, and set attainable goals in order to see a marketable product that is both pleasing to the Lord and interesting to the public.

To Self-publish or Not to Self-publish

Before you choose to self-publish, you must realistically evaluate your situation:

* ❖ Do you have the financial ability to risk publishing on your own? I made it a personal goal to have cash in hand before I published. I did not want to make a mistake that my family would suffer from.

* ❖ Do you have the organizational and time-management skills necessary to write? Do you have the stamina and discipline to complete what you begin? The Lord warns us to "count the cost" before we begin a work. It will take hours upon hours of your time, can you commit to it?

* ❖ Can you prioritize and set positive, realistic goals for yourself? If you are a procrastinator, now is the time to change those habits!

* ❖ Do you have people that can help you edit? You don't want someone who thinks that everything you do is "just wonderful." You want someone you can trust to tell you the honest truth about what you have written. You want someone with the expertise to catch even the slightest grammatical errors. One professor paid his students for each error they were able to find in the textbook he had written. Not a bad idea!

Now that you have answered all of those questions in the affirmative, you know what you are going to write about, and you know how you're going to pursue publication, it's time to write!

Chapter 5

Getting Ready To Write

Many people who want to write a book have the ability, but they aren't sure where to begin the process, they are not organized enough to complete the project, or they are not self motivated enough to follow through with the task. This chapter provides practical information to assist you in getting started by organizing your material and beginning the writing process.

Where to Begin

The best place to begin your project is in the presence of God. When you have a close, personal, daily communion with Jesus you can feel His heartbeat. When you pray, you sense what it is He wants you to do. If you feel you have an idea, ask for His divine direction in the matter and then wait for His answer. When you feel His leading, proceed.

To keep things manageable and in perspective, concentrate on one subject at a time. Break the project into smaller pieces and it will appear more manageable and realistic. One day you might do research. The next day you might "map" a chapter (an easy way to outline will be shared in Chapter 6). Another day you might design the back-cover or work on the appendix. The key is to develop a plan and work on it each day if possible, or at least set aside a number of hours per week to write. A reasonable goal would be to write 1000 words a day or two to three pages.

As you begin your writing, consider your print deadline. If you are trying to have your book completed by a particular date so it can be included in a catalog, or to enable you to make your books available for sale at a particular meeting, keep those dates in mind. Depending on the printer's work load, you will need to allow at least six to eight weeks printing time. If possible, it is good to allow an additional couple of weeks in order to iron out any problems should they arise. Rush jobs cost you more money and often make for mistakes.

Work Space and Tools

Organize your workspace. Make your home office a pleasant place. You don't need to go out and buy a big beautiful desk with all the matching bookcases, but you do need a place that you can call your own. You need a place where you can spread out your papers. Something out of the way from the general traffic pattern works best for most people, preferably a place where you can close the door. Many famous authors began writing on a desk put together by placing a door over two filing cabinets. Don't let the lack of fancy equipment keep you from writing.

In the survey I mentioned, Nan Pamer stated that she takes her laptop computer to a local deli a couple of times a week and spends two or three hours writing. In the hustle and bustle of that atmosphere she finds the best time to write. I need quiet uninterrupted time to write. This just proves we all have different needs! Find a place that works best for **you**.

If you don't have a computer, get one. You don't need to buy the most up to date one on the market. Your main concern is desktop publishing capabilities and an older model would be fine for this.

There are several computer programs that are good to use to prepare your manuscript. This book was done with Microsoft Word®, which several authors in my survey indicated they used. Pagemaker®, Microsoft Works®, Adobe Pagemaker®, and QuarkXPress® were also mentioned as being beneficial to their writing. It is best to use a program you are already familiar with rather than purchase a new program and have to take time to learn it.

Quick Verse® by Parsons, and P.C. Study Bible 3®, are great programs to help you find scriptures and insert them in your manuscript. These programs have other resources such as Bible dictionaries, concordances and atlases to help you with your research.

You also need a printer to allow you to print copies for editing purposes. Your printer doesn't matter until you are ready to do your final "camera-ready copy." This is the copy you send to the book printer. As you are writing and editing, a standard ink jet printer is fine, but your final copy must be as clear and clean as possible and that can only be obtained from a laser printer with 600 dpi or better. To the natural eye, ink jet print looks fine, but when it is copied, it looks fuzzy. Compare print from each of them and you will see the difference.

Again, don't feel you need to purchase a laser printer. You can save your work to a disk, CD or zip disk and take it to a friend's house to print or to one of the infamous printing stations available today. Several office supply stores offer these services and they are much cheaper than it would cost for you to purchase your own printer. You may even be able to use a computer lab facility at a local tech school or college.

Motivation

For the most part, the determination and motivation have to come from you. If you treat your writing like it is an assignment from the Lord, you will be more apt to take the necessary time for it! Setting goals and developing a tentative timetable will help you stay on schedule and keep you moving in the right direction.

Develop discipline in your writing. As you sit down to write each day, set a goal as to how many pages or chapters you will complete that day. Avoid getting up to get something to drink, water the plants, clean off your desk, pay bills, or look at catalogs. Procrastination has destroyed many wonderful intentions.

If you hit what some call "writer's block," read for a while. Good writers are typically avid readers. Often times, without even realizing it, we pick up the writing style of our favorite author. Reading just a couple of pages of their writing may be just what you need to get going.

You must believe in yourself and set reasonable goals to make your book a reality. Believing you can do it is half of the battle. Daily, encourage yourself in your ability to write, knowing that with the help of the Lord, all things are possible!

The more you write, the better you will become at writing. There is an old saying that says, "If you can say it, you can write it." Pretend you are 'talking' with a friend. Write clearly and crisply.

Write what you know from your own experiences and from your research. That's what people want. They want something they can relate to, something that they know is real. Be **real**. Allow the reader to feel your emotions. Allow the reader the opportunity to see that you make mistakes and to see how God helps you through them. None of us are perfect, but we are striving to be perfected. As we share our lives with others, we help to perfect them.

To be real, you do not need to share the graphic details of sin nor do you need to write in a manner that would embarrass people. Also, it is best not to use the names of people unless it shows them in a favorable light.

Hopefully, by now, you know what you will be writing about and you have already begun your research. Now it's time to:

- ❖ Set a goal as to when you will finish your research and begin writing.
- ❖ Decide how much you will write per week or how much time you will spend writing each week.
- ❖ Decide which avenue you will pursue in publication and begin getting information as to their requirements.
- ❖ Take a look at the objectives in the timetable at the end of this chapter and adapt it to your own needs.
- ❖ Seek God's perfect will in your life and ask Him to help you complete this work.

If you truly believe the Lord is prompting you to do this work, make it a point not to let Him down! With His help you can do all things!

Suggested Timetable

Task: **Projected completion date:**

Initiation: Getting Started
Evaluate the motivation for
writing a book.

Develop a plan for writing, publishing
and marketing.

Inspiration: Book Idea
Write a statement detailing
what I want the reader to learn
or obtain by reading my book.

Decide on a place and time
to write.

Develop a timeline.

Preparation: Research
Set up a work area.

Set up a binder.

Gather research.

Develop an outline of my book.
(tentative table of contents)

Organize my material with the
"pilot system." (More information about this is found in Chapter 6.)

Contact those whose input I need for editing, cover copy.

Do necessary research into actual mode of publication to pursue.
Decide who will typeset, edit and print it.

Perspiration: Writing
Complete first rough draft of the book.

Content edit.

Fill in the gaps

Verification: Final Editing for Accuracy
Give chapters to peers for editing.

Publication: Production and Promotion
Send off to printer or publisher.

Write query letters to publishing houses if following traditional route, and to sales outlets if self-publishing.

Chapter 6

How to Write A Book

When I wrote my first book, *A Time to Grow...,* I packed up the manuscript and sent it off just as I began taking a Christian writing course. It didn't take long for me to realize I had basically done everything wrong! I immediately prayed that somehow it would get lost in the mail so I would have the opportunity to "do it right!" Evidently my prayer was answered because they said they never received it. This allowed me the opportunity to clean up some editorial errors, write autobiography material, query the publisher properly and to send in a polished manuscript. In other words, to look professional.

As a Christian author, I think sometimes that because we feel we have "received something from the Lord," we think that everyone else should just accept it. Christian editors have received illegibly handwritten articles and manuscripts on stained napkins, cardboard shirt forms and on the backs of envelopes, and the author wonders why the editor won't publish their work! We may have truly 'received something from the Lord,' but we still need to present it in the best possible light and witness that we can. You never know where your book will end up or who will read it one day!

If you choose to self-publish you won't have to worry about some of the things I've mentioned, such as querying an editor, but there is a myriad of other details that you must consider. This chapter will assist you in putting some of these issues in perspective.

Your manuscript needs to be logically organized. If you are writing a novel, the story line usually dictates the order. If you are doing nonfiction it may be more difficult to organize your material in a logical sequence. You need a simple system to help you break the manuscript into small, easy-to-attack chunks, so you will not feel overwhelmed by the project.

The Pilot System

Dan Poynter, the most frequently quoted self-published author today, teaches what he calls "the pilot system," which is an excellent system to use when writing a nonfiction book. It is a system designed to help you organize your material in a cohesive and logical sequence.

Gather all your notes and research. Use scissors to cut the pages up so that each sheet of paper has notes or research on only one particular subject. You will need a lot of space for this next step so go to an area where you can spread out. A large table or the floor works well for this.

Take into account all of the subjects you intend to cover and roughly divide your message into 10 to 12 subject areas. Write these topics or subjects on Post-it Notes or 3 x 5 cards. Lay these labels out on the floor or table and begin going through each scrap of paper and placing it in the most appropriate pile. The labels don't necessarily need to be in the same order that your table of contents will follow. It might be easier if the labels are placed in alphabetical order.

Spreading the material out helps you to see how the whole project relates to each individual section. Move the piles around to insure that you have a logical flow of thought and to avoid duplicating material. (Mapping your work, found later in this chapter, is a tool that can help you label and organize your material.)

Then go through all your notes, underlining important points and jotting down additional thoughts. Cut and paste your notes together in a logical sequence. Read the whole section of pasted-together notes to get a feel for the overall theme. As you begin the writing process, develop your thoughts by adding your own observations, experiences and stories. This will provide you with the meat for an entire chapter.

After you finish, draw up a preliminary table of contents as you logically sequence your material. Then sort through all your notes and research materials and "pile it" (pilot) in the appropriate "chapter" or section.

When the notes are in what appears to be the appropriate pile, look for the common denominators. How does everything fit together? This will help you in determining what you should use for chapter titles and sub-headings within your chapters.

After deciding on chapter titles, cut and paste all the material you have gathered on a particular subject, into that "chapter." As you organize the material and begin tying it together, you will probably have more thoughts on the subject, jot them down and add them. If you find that there are some thin areas, you may need to do more research. Chapters don't have to be the same length, but you don't want one or two page chapters and thirty-five page chapters. Try to balance out your material.

What to Write First

It is not necessary to begin writing your book at page one. You can begin writing any chapter you feel led to. Just make sure when you compile it, the sequence of chapters makes sense. Write the chapter you are most excited about. It will help to propel you into the project with a sense of excitement. Since chapter one is essentially the introduction, it may even be better to write it later when you have an overall feel for where the book is going.

Setting Up a Binder

After you have done this initial organization and assessment of information, there are a couple of ways you may choose to keep your materials organized. One way is to keep each chapter in a separate manila folder. Another way is to store them in an accordion folder, one chapter in each section. Once you begin typing your manuscript, a wonderful way to store pages that have been printed out, is in a three-ring binder with clear pockets in the front and back. You can make mock-up pages to serve as your covers and place them in the clear plastic pockets on the front and back of the binder. As you print out the pages and place them in the binder, you get the feeling that your book is progressing. In the binder, your project becomes portable and you are free to carry it with you, do editing and add additional material as you see the need. It also helps other people to realize that you are indeed "writing a book!"

Typesetting

As you begin keyboarding your material it is best to set up your pages with the same margins that your book printer requires. (This is another good reason to decide early in the process, what print avenue you will take.) If you are sending your manuscript to a traditional publisher, you do not need to worry about typesetting but you will need to follow standard manuscript submission guidelines. This will give you a feel for what your book will look like. It will also help you judge the number of words that will fit on a page and give you a fair approximation of the length your book.

As you keyboard, try to complete one section at a time. This will make it easier to be consistent with margins and fonts. Keep a style sheet or guide by your computer that lists the font name, size and number of spaces for each chapter heading. Note whether the font is bold or italicized. This will help the entire book to look consistent.

I have tried two different ways to type and set up a book. For *Growing in All the Right Places*, I saved each chapter in a separate file and then pulled them together into one file at the end. Then I numbered the pages. In this book I have tried to type straight through the book, setting up the pages as I go. The best advice I can give you is to know the capabilities of your software. Your software is filled with all sorts of tools to help you, but you need to know how to tap into them.

Hopefully you have a good idea as to how you will ultimately publish your book. As a self-publisher, you will save yourself a lot of time, energy and money if you know the specific requirements of your publisher or printer before you type your manuscript. Some book printers require that everything be sent to them on disk and in a particular word processing program. Others want only camera ready copy. Do your homework.

Keep a pen and paper with you at all times. Once you begin your project, at the least expected times you will have the most awesome thoughts cross your mind that will be wonderful material to add to your book. Write them down immediately while the impact and memory is fresh. If you try to remember later you may forget the specifics and lose some powerful insight.

As you continue to think and take notes, add them to the appropriate chapters. Delete material that doesn't really fit and fine tune your writing. Look for continuity, duplication and clear organization. Try to think of questions that the reader may have as he or she reads your book. Explain things as if you are talking with a friend who is new to the subject. Write like you speak, write clearly. Don't use big words when small ones will do. Gone are the days of superfluous words and lengthy, adjective filled sentences that take a college dictionary to interpret! People want to be able to understand what they read. Entire books have been written to teach people how to write memos that say what they mean in the fewest number of words.

As you write, vary your sentence length and your paragraph length. Today, shorter is better. Make your sentences direct and to the point. Use descriptive adjectives and nouns. Avoid passive sentences that tend to drag on. Make sure all the sentences in a paragraph relate to each other. Use transitions to move from one paragraph to the next.

Mapping

Mapping is a tool for assisting and enhancing your writing, It is a process by which you brainstorm and organize your thoughts and research before actually beginning to write. You can use mapping to set up the chapters in a book, to organize thoughts for an individual chapter or to write an article or essay.

To begin a "Map," write the main idea in the center of the page. It may be a key word, a phrase, or a couple of main thoughts you want to pull together. (Example 1.)

Next, place related ideas on spokes, or branches, that radiate from this central idea. (Example 2.) These branches become your paragraphs.

Add details to the spokes. (Example 3)

Number the branches (paragraphs) in a logical sequence to organize your information. (Example 4.)

Additional keys to mapping:

❖ Before you begin the mapping/brainstorming process, you may want to make a list of thoughts you already have.

❖ Use unlined paper so existing lines do not distract you.

❖ Make your points brief. You want to put everything on one sheet of paper. (You will develop them into paragraphs later in the process.)

❖ As you get a new idea, draw a spoke that touches your original line.

❖ Now brainstorm your thoughts. Don't worry about organizing them. At this point, your goal is to get all your thoughts down on paper

❖ Write down everything you can think of that relates to your topic. Don't worry about editing at this time. This process of brainstorming will help you to bring several inspirational ideas to the forefront.

❖ When you finish, look over what you have written. See if there are any gaps in your material.

Advantages of mapping:

❖ Mapping helps you clearly define the central idea of your writing. Because you position it in the middle of the page, all connecting lines will relate to your basic topic.

❖ Mapping allows you to see all your basic information on one page.

❖ It allows you to add new information without messy crossing out or squeezing in.

❖ You are able to see all your information in on one page, so you are better able to logically sequence your composition without leaving out valuable information.

Example 1:

Self-publishing

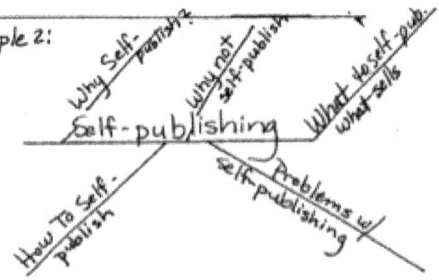

Example 2:

Example 3:

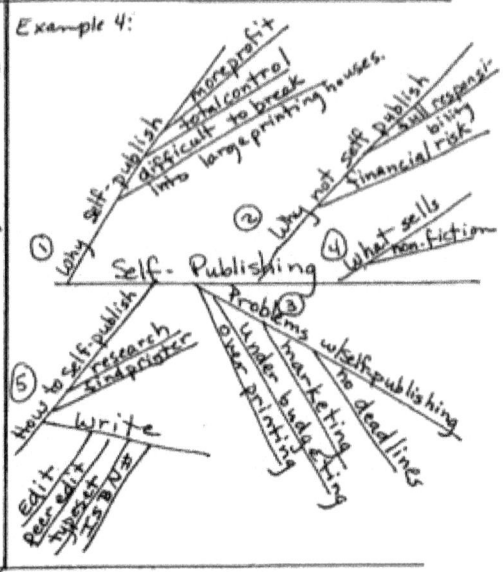

Example 4:

41

Chapter 7

Write Tight

"Write Tight" is a recently coined phrase that means: to write clearly enough to get your point across with the least amount of words. Today people want information compacted so it takes them less time to absorb it. Writing instructors are encouraging people to write with short words rather than long ones and to avoid cliches.

As you begin your project, write a mission statement. Take some time to sit down and evaluate what it is you want to accomplish through the writing of your book. Writing a mission statement will help you to stay focused on your subject matter, to write tight, and keep you from "chasing rabbits" (getting off on subjects that are unrelated to the topic). Your mission statement might end up being your **Foreword**, or good copy material for the back of your book.

As you write your mission statement, consider whom it is that will read your book. Knowing your audience will determine how you write. It will help you to write in a language and style that the reader understands. If you are writing to new converts you will write differently than if you are writing to ministers. Anticipate the reader's questions and try to address them in your writing.

Next, write the introduction. This sets the stage for the entire book. It tells the scope of the book, the material that will be covered, and how the reader will benefit from reading it. Writing the **Introduction** early in the project will also help you to maintain your focus.

After your book is finished, you may need to revise your introduction to incorporate additional information that you may not have anticipated. As you write, the Holy Spirit will bring things to your remembrance that you failed to think of when you began your project. There are times when you will feel completely overwhelmed by the power of God as He works through you. Allow Jesus to anoint you as you write and follow His leading. He knows who will eventually read what you have written. What an awesome responsibility we have to convey the word of truth to the world!

You may already have most of the material you need to write a book. Have you written any articles or done any speaking? My first two books on Spiritual growth were basically all from messages I had spoken. They needed to be rewritten to address a reader rather than an audience and organized and refreshed with newer stories, but the heart of each book was basically complete when I began the books.

As you write, use anecdotes to help convey your message. Anecdotes are stories that you yourself may have experienced, or you have heard or read about. They help to illustrate and clarify the point you are trying to make. They make your writing come alive and add a note of interest. Jesus taught in parables, stories that the listeners easily related to. When people read what you have written and connect with your experiences, they are in a position to make changes in their own lives. They realize they are not alone in their thinking or problem and that there is a solution.

For your book to make a difference in the lives of others, you must be willing to share your heart. We have all had struggles, tests and trials that Jesus has graciously seen us through. The ministry comes when you are willing to share how Jesus has helped you to be an overcomer. It gives the reader hope. They identify with you as a real person and realize they can also be overcomers. Writing in a realm that exists without problems or boasts of always being above problems is surreal.

Contrary to some popular teaching, we don't always live "on the mountain." Oftentimes our greatest growth comes as a result of the "valley" experiences. By sharing your "valley" experiences as well as your victories you give people a balanced view of the Christian life. You may even save someone from having to go through what you have gone through by helping him or her to make wise decisions.

Again, don't share the gory details of your life that can be offensive to the reader and don't mention the names of people that may be offended or embarrassed by a story you tell. The situation may be true and although it has been forgiven, it can still hurt. It is best to tell these "valley" stories in the third person, as though it happened to someone else and you are merely relaying it to the reader.

Fiction

Fiction writers have several points to consider in their writing. The book must have a strong plot that is believable and appropriate to the genre. It might be helpful to read Lawrence Block's *Writing the Novel*, which is said to have a good overview of fiction methods.

It is important to alleviate confusion in the story line. The story needs a well-defined theme with a clear message so it is easy to follow. Watch the verb tense as you write, as well as each character's point of view, and make them consistent throughout.

Characters should seem real, having qualities that make us identify with them. Take the time to do a character sketch for each character. Detail every conceivable thing you can think about them. Age, sex and physical descriptions are important, however; mannerisms, personality, education, family background, religious background, passions and pet peeves are important as well. Once **you** know your characters well, it will be easier to make them come alive for the reader.

Settings must be thoroughly researched to be realistic. Appeal to the senses as you write. Allow the reader to see and hear the character's surroundings through good description.

Dialogue often hinges on the setting and is extremely important in fiction writing. It must be authentic as it moves the story along and adds depth to the characters. Remember people use slang when they talk as well as contractions. Read your dialogue aloud to see if it makes sense.

Book Length

To be considered a book, there must be a minimum of 50 pages. Anything smaller is considered a booklet or a pamphlet. If you are writing a standard, perfect bound book, you should try to have between 130 and 280 typeset pages in a 5.5" x 8.5" book.

When a book is printed, it is printed on several very large sheets of paper, which are folded into what is called "signatures." Depending on the size of the press, there are generally 32 signatures. This means that 16 of the pages will be printed on one side of the sheet and 16 will be printed on the other side. Because of this, you need to figure the pages of your book in multiples of 32.

To visualize how this works, take a sheet of paper and fold it in half four times. What you will have is 16 panels on each side of the sheet (16 up and 16 down) which equals 32 pages in the signature. If your book ends up being 176 pages, it will have 5 signatures of 32 pages and one signature of 16 (which simply means the press stopped at half the count).

As you typeset, you should set your margins as they will be when the book is printed, then you will have a better idea as to how many pages it will end up being. Remember, every page counts in the printing process, even if it is blank and has no number on it. To accommodate the signatures, the printer will add blank pages to the end of your book to equal the multiple of 16. To avoid excessive blank pages you might want to add additional material or even pages for notes to be written in. Since you will be paying for the pages you might as well fill them with something of interest to the reader. If your book goes one page into the next signature, you may consider cutting something out, because the overall printing price is based on the number of signatures per book.

Make sure you give your reader genuine value. A recent trend to expand the size of a book includes the use of large fonts. Large fonts do not add to the overall general appeal of the book. In some cases, it simply makes the book look cheap.

Chapter 8

Is It a Book Yet?

By now you are probably wondering, "When will this really be a book?" If you are following the Pilot System, hopefully your book is taking shape as you organize it in your notebook. Setting up the binder in the same order you want the book to be will keep you organized and save you time. You can make additions and revisions as you go.

Title

Have you settled on a title yet? Some people have trouble coming up with a title for their book while others know their title years before they begin writing. For many it is difficult to sum their material up in just a few choice words.

The best titles are catchy phrases that have a ring to them. Make your title specific, familiar and short. Some examples of catchy words to use in titles of "how to books" are: guide, complete, new, manual, handbook, etc. Use descriptive words that let the reader know what they will find in your book. Come up with a good "one liner" which tells a complete and compelling story about your book.

If you haven't decided on a final title, at least develop a working title to use while you are writing. As you work on your book, you can brainstorm a list of titles and subtitles and test them on your friends and family members. As you share possible titles with others, record their reactions.

Nonfiction books often have a title as well as a subtitle to further describe the content of the book. The subtitle is longer than the title and should be more descriptive. Dan Poynter, says you shouldn't go over 92 characters in your title, even with the subtitle. Others say you need to count syllables in your title and that limiting your main title to five or seven syllables is most effective.

Eye Appeal

Once you've started writing and have your material organized, you can begin to think of the final product. What will your book look like?

What your book looks like is crucial to its marketability. "Your cover will either sell your book, or kill sales,"says Athena Dean, author of *You CanDo It!* You do not want your book to look like it is self-published. You want to develop a product that rivals any traditionally published book. Bookstore browsers spend approximately eight seconds on the front cover, and fifteen seconds on the back cover. That gives your book only a few seconds of consideration. Your book cover must arrest their attention from thousands of other volumes available and convince them that your book is the one they should buy. Take a trip through the aisles of your local Christian bookstore and see what is selling.

Find a book that is similar in nature to the one you are writing. You may want to purchase it so you can dissect it to see how it is put together. Note the cover design, the half-title page, the title page and the table of contents. What font did they use on the cover? What color scheme did they use? Note the information found on the copyright page. Note the use of testimonials on the inside of the book or on the back cover. Take a look at the dedication page, and the foreword, if it has one. Does it have a page for acknowledgments? Does it have an introduction? Take a look at the back of the book. Does it have a glossary or an index? Is there an appendix? Is there an order blank to make it easier for the reader to obtain other materials that the author has available for sale? These are all very important issues to consider as your book begins to take shape.

Registering Your Book

Now is a good time to apply for your ISBN number. ISBN stands for: International Standard Book Number. It is an essential identifying number used for ordering and cataloging purposes. Although not required for self-publishers to obtain, it does allow your book to be catalogued in a system that would allow anyone in the world to procure a copy, and makes your book available through every book distributor in the world.

You can apply on-line for your ISBN number at www.bowker.com, or you can download the forms and mail them in. Keep in mind, as I stated earlier, at the current time you their requirements state that you must purchase a minimum of ten numbers.

When you apply for this number, you are applying as a bonefide publisher. They will require you to have a name for your publishing company. If you know that you will be writing more books, this may be the best thing for you to do. However, if you are unsure whether purchasing ten numbers is worth the need for one number, or if you are not sure you want to become a publisher, you may want to go through a small publishing house like myself.

If you will note on the copyright page, The Ready Scribe® published this particular book. This is the name of my publishing house. If a person in Japan wanted to purchase a copy of one of my works or books, they could contact me through the ISBN number that indicates The Ready Scribe as the publisher. If you go on-line to look for a copy of either book, it will inform you that you can contact The Ready Scribe to purchase a copy.

If you pick up a copy of *Writer's Market* you will find that there are many small publishers, like myself, that publish only one or two books per year. [Basically, being "the publisher" just allows you to control how long your book remains available.]

This would also be a good time to apply for your copyright. The copyright protects your written work so that others may not claim it as their own material. [Like the ISBN number, it helps to insure that you are the identifiable author of the work.] The copyright term lasts for the life of the author, plus fifty years after his or her death.

You can find out more information about copyright laws by calling the U.S. Copyright Office at 202-707-9100 or by checking on-line at http://lcweb.loc.gov. To obtain the copyright application form (Form TX) you can call 202-707-9100 or download them from this web-site: http:lcweb.loc.gov/copyright.

You must be sure to print the copyright notice in the proper form. If this isn't done correctly, the copyright may not be valid. When you type your copyright page, make sure you use the symbol © (which secures your legal rights), the year, and your name as the copyright holder. You also need to include the terms "All Rights Reserved," and "Printed in the United States of America," plus "First Printing" and the year. As you print later editions, change the copyright page to indicate the number of printings.

By law, if your book is printed after September first of one year, you may use the next calendar year as your copyright date. If your book is to be printed September 10, 2003, you are legally able to state that the publishing date is 2004. This allows the author to have a couple of extra months before the book becomes a year old.

Something I was unaware of before my research, is that titles are not subject to copyright. When you copyright your book, you are protecting the material **in** your book, not the title. Another interesting note is that you don't have to apply for the copyright right away. You can apply after the book is published and it will still be registered. Even if you don't register with the Copyright Office, your work is copyright protected if you use the symbol correctly.

Setting Up Your Book

The inside of your book will have three basic parts. Preliminary pages called "front matter," the text or the body of your book, and the "back matter".

Take a close look at the book you have chosen to dissect. As you open the cover you will see a blank page facing you on the right side. When you turn the page you will see that it is also blank on the backside. The next page (on the right) is considered the half title page. It may have the title and the subtitle but that is probably all you will see. On the backside of that page there may be a list of other books written by the same author. Otherwise it is probably blank too. The next page is the Title page that includes the full title and subtitle as well as the author's name and the publisher. Note that it is on the right hand side of the page (recto).

On the back of the title page, verso (the left-hand side), you will find the copyright page. Look at it carefully. Note how it is set up, especially if you are doing your own typesetting. The copyright page is the most important page in the book. Proofread it a dozen times. It has the copyright notice, printing history (the number of printings and revisions) the ISBN number, the name and address of the publisher, and it tells where it was printed. Those who know the book trade will turn to the copyright page first when picking up a book. Next to the cover, it is the most important part of the book. It must look professional. If it doesn't, the reader may decide the entire book may not be worth reading.

If you reprint your book, make sure you change the copyright page to reflect the second printing or revision so the reader knows it is up-to-date. A second printing lets the reader know that sales have been good and that the book may have something he or she is interested in.

The next couple of pages are up to the discretion of the author and vary from book to book. Some people have a page of "Acknowledgement" or "Dedication". This can be a great sales tool. If you list everyone who helped you with the production of the book, people will be interested in purchasing it because they had a part in it. To make sure you don't forget anyone, keep a sheet and add names to it as you go.

Because of our sue happy society, many authors put a disclaimer in the front of their book so the reader cannot come back on the author if he or she feels they did not get sound advice from the book.

Some authors include an introduction to share pertinent information with the reader and to help them better understand the purpose for writing the book.

You may decide to have a foreword in your book. The foreword is basically an endorsement of your work and credibility that is written by someone else.

The table of contents is usually found before the introduction or foreword. It always begins on the right hand side of the page. It should include the chapter titles, chapter numbers, and the beginning page numbers of each chapter. You can typeset your table of contents as you put your book together and add the specific page numbers later when the book is formatted.

Chapter titles need to be as clear as possible. They should summarize the chapter. Titles can have subheadings to clarify their content. The potential reader will skim the titles to see if there is anything that he or she needs.

Then comes the text. Start your book off with an action chapter. Give it the best you've got! Chapter one should entice the reader and wet his or her appetite. New writers want to begin with "the beginning" and put a boring history chapter first. Use chapter one to draw the reader into your book. If the reader finds something intriguing in the first chapter, he or she will read on.

As you begin typesetting your pages, make a style sheet that lists the font name and size of type used for each title, heading and sub-heading and whether it is bold, italicized or underlined. Also, note how many spaces are left between each line of print, and what font sizes the spaces are. This will save you a lot of time and frustration as you check to make sure that your entire book is consistent in style.

As you are typesetting, always begin new chapters on the right hand side (recto page). Drop down the page about one-third of the way from the top of the page to write the chapter number and title. Use a larger font for the chapter number and still larger font for the chapter titles. Make sure you put them in bold type so that they stand out. Usually the titles and headings are centered on the page, but it is up to you. Again, look at your example for guidance.

Try to avoid having only one or two sentences on the last page of a chapter (widows pages). It just looks better when there is more print on the page.

Keep in mind that when your book is being numbered; even the blank pages are included in the numbering. As you set the numbering in your typesetting, you can choose to not have a number on the blank pages, but remember they are still a part of the page count in a book.

Then comes the third section: the back matter. This can include a glossary, appendix, index, bibliography, footnotes and an order blank for reorders.

The glossary is useful to explain terms you have included in your book. The terms must be in alphabetical order.

The appendix may include important lists and resources you have added to make your book a reference tool that readers will come back to.

The index lists key words and phrases found in your book and the page numbers where the information is located. List all main headings, subheadings and key words in the index. Cross reference similar terms. Example: Vanity publishing. (*See* Subsidy publishing).

Some computer programs have indexing features that can do most of the work for you, if yours does not have this feature, read through your book and use 3" by 5" cards to jot down key words and important phrases. Once on 3" by 5" cards they will be easier to alphabetize. The index should be formatted in two columns and in alphabetical order.

If you update your book and reprint it, make sure you revise the index because the page numbers will have changed.

You may want to include an order blank in the back of your book. The reader may have borrowed the book from the library or a friend and would like his or her own copy. This also gives you the opportunity to offer additional books or tapes you may have that the reader is unaware of. Make sure you list the full price of the book including sales tax and shipping. Again, if you revise your book and the price has gone up, this page will need to be changed as well.

If you set up a binder, make sure that you include a sheet for each of these sections and add material to it as you go, that way you won't forget anything.

Chapter 9

Your Best Advertising Tool: The Cover

You may already have a mental picture of what you want your cover design to be, or you may not have any idea how you would like it to look. Whatever the case, keep in mind, your cover is your billboard. It is your greatest advertisement. Whether it is laying on a table or standing upright on a bookshelf, it must be attractive and professional.

Because book browsers give a book only a few seconds of consideration, the cover must grab their attention enough for them to pick it up and take a closer look. You must hook them quickly and convince them that your book has the answers they are looking for or the story they want to read.

As you look through the Christian bookstore, what grabs and holds your attention? What do the covers of the best sellers look like? What do they say on the back? How is the material set up?

I found it very helpful to look through the Christian book club catalogs to find covers that appealed to me. The blurb on the flier gives a brief summary of the book and can give you an idea how to summarize the material in your book to use for your back cover or for advertising purposes.

What made you choose the particular book that you dissected earlier in this chapter? Look closely at the cover. Were you drawn to the font style? Was it a color combination or a picture? Was it the design layout? Was it the title? Or was it the author? How is the cover set up?

The entire outer cover is important, including the spine. Booksellers say books sell five times faster when they are displayed face-out but we know we can't count on them being displayed that way. In a bookstore or the library, most books are shelved with the spine out. This narrow strip is your first sales tool. It is the book's first introduction to the public. The spine displays the title of the book, the author and the publisher. It must stand out in some way to attract the reader. Put the title near the top of the cover and don't say "by" for the author. The font on the spine should be plain and bold so it is easy to read. Make sure the print runs the right way and that it is large enough to see from a reasonable distance. The color of the print should stand out and contrast with the color of the cover.

Some book printers offer stock cover designs for free. However, unless you are a well-established writer, steer clear of these prefab covers. Their designs are generic and they typically do not reflect your subject matter. Believe me, best selling authors do not rely on stock covers to sell their books. Do your homework well. This is where many self-publishers fail and their books appear amateurish.

Book printers can help you with cover art. They charge a fee per hour, but if you give them specific information and examples of what you are looking for, you will efficiently utilize artistic design time. For my last book, *Growing in All the Right Places*, I went through graphics programs and printed out six photos I liked. They went through their available art files and e-mailed eight pictures that were similar to what I originally sent them. From their offerings, I selected a photo to be used for my cover.

I sent them the picture of a book whose lettering style and layout I liked and in less than an hour's worth of artistic design time, I had the perfect cover.

Make your cover reflect the essence of your book. The font, typestyle, whether bold, block or fancy and the photo or illustration you use, must be slanted to your reader's interest and go along with the theme of the book. If the book is for men, let the cover reflect masculinity. If it is for women, make it look feminine. I know one writer who used different colored covers for the same book. She noted that it was interesting who purchased which color! By making the covers different colors, different people were attracted to different covers and she sold more books.

Be careful not to let the artwork overpower the lettering. The title should be the first thing you see when you look at the cover. The title should literally pop off the background and be capable of being seen from a distance.

Another thing to think about when designing your cover is how will it look printed in black and white on a copy machine? If you intend to do a mailing to advertise your book, you want the copy to be clear.

If your book printer doesn't have an in-house cover designing, then you need to get in touch with a professional graphic arts person. Share with the artist the theme of your book, show him or her, the table of contents and at least two sample chapters so they have a better understanding of what you need your cover to reflect. Make sure you discuss how much the artwork will cost. You need to budget for it. Make sure you deal with someone who has had experience working with book manufacturers and who knows how to prepare the final artwork or electronic files for a book printer.

Morris Press has an entire booklet designed to assist you in designing your own cover with the help of various layouts, fonts and the availability of their in-house graphic artists at reasonable fees. I'm sure there are other book printers that offer similar services.

Cover Copy

"Copy" is what is actually written on your book's cover. The non-fiction book usually has the title and a subtitle on the front cover. The back cover may have testimonials written by people who have given you feedback as you shared chapters of your book with them or it may simply highlight the information that you have included in the book. These are called cover blurbs and they are the sales message. This is where you promote your book and to a degree, yourself.

Testimonies from people who have read your book give it greater credibility and sales appeal, especially if it is a well-known person. If you have a foreword written by an expert in your field, include their name on the front. This also brings respect to your work.

You should also include a biographical section. List your accomplishments, honors, awards, degrees, experiences and past writings to establish you as an authority on the subject you are writing about. When people see that you actually have the experiences and credentials to write on a particular subject, they are more likely to purchase your book. You may even want to include a picture.

You may want to write your back cover copy before you write your book. It will help you focus your audience and what they want or need. You can state why you are writing the book and list the benefits the reader will glean from your book. The cover and back have a dramatic impact on the books review potential and sales record. If your book is reviewed, often the reviewer will use exactly what you have written on your back cover.

On your back cover, you need to leave room for the bar code, should you choose to have one. For your book to be sold in most markets, a bar code is needed. The bar code includes the ISBN number for cataloging and inventory purposes and it can include the price. Some bookstores may not require it and will simply put their own sticker on the book if you do not have a bar code, but other stores may not carry the book without the code.

There are companies that you can pay to develop a bar code for you or your book printer may be able to take care of that detail for you. Most books have this code at the bottom of the book.

Again, take a look at best selling book covers. What do they say on the back? How do they encourage the browser to purchase the book? What do they promise the reader that they will receive from reading the book?

I found it helpful to peruse through several books to see how they were set up. Choose one of your favorites and look at it closely.

As you open the front cover, are there any blank pages? If it is a paperback (perfect bound) book, you will probably see a page on the right hand side (recto) that has nothing but the title. On the back (verso) you will find a blank page, then another recto page with the title, author and publisher. This is the official "title page." Behind it is the copyright page, which includes the copyright data, the ISBN number and other information regarding the production and classification of the book.

The next recto page is probably the table of contents. Then you may see various items of "front matter." There may be a note of thanks, a forward, a disclaimer, an introduction, or it may go directly into the first chapter.

Note carefully the set up of the book. The table of contents and the first page of a chapter, all begin on the recto side of the page. If a chapter ends on a recto page, simply skip the next page to allow the next chapter to begin on the next recto page.

Note what items are at the end of the book, "book matter." The appendix, an order blank, the index and the glossary are all found at the end of the book.

Hopefully by now, you are seeing your book take shape.

Chapter 10

How Many Times do I Have to Edit This Thing?

If you are a beginning writer, you will find that your manuscript becomes your baby. You industriously labor long hours over it. You sweat over it. You may even cry over it. It becomes a living, breathing part of you. You read it over and over, grooming it with a fine-toothed comb. You are sure it is perfect. Finally you garner the courage to ask a friend or loved one to proof it for you...

Unfortunately, as anointed as we may feel when we write, there is still room for improvement! Allowing others to edit your book is a necessary part of the process. You must learn to accept the fact that not all the words you write are crucial and that some things may be best said in a different way or left out entirely. James Michener says he invites four editors to "tear up his manuscript." (I don't think my skin is **that** thick yet!)

I would much rather have someone catch a mistake in my manuscript than have the book manufacturer print 1,000 copies like I did with my first printing of *Growing in All the Right Places*! At the last minute, I had to revise the table of contents, so I typed it up and sent it in without having someone else review it. In my retype, "Returning to First Love" became "Returning to **Fist** Love"! Mind you, the chapter is about restoring love in your personal relationships! You can only imagine my horror when I opened the first of twenty-one boxes and found that typo! Interestingly enough, since it is near the bottom of the page, few people have commented on it, but I know it's there.

When you give someone your work to proofread or edit, don't take his or her corrections personally. Realize they are attempting to help you improve your writing. They are trying to help you produce your very best work. Don't become defensive. Remember, they are **not** criticizing you, they are critiquing something you wrote.

Sometimes it is easier to ask a friend to edit for you or to pay a professional editor rather than have a family member edit. To this day, I don't have my husband help me with editing. My daughters help me, but his first read is when it comes off the press!

Stanley Schmidt, a writer for Writer's Digest, quoted his brother as saying, "The trouble with computers is that they make it too easy for bad writing to look good." Schmidt, who edits professionally, noted that when he started editing, amateur manuscripts were often recognizable at a glance. They were single-spaced in faded ink and every third word was misspelled, or they were submitted hand-scribbled in purple ink on orange paper. He said, "Now they are more likely to be neatly laser-printed on one side of white paper, with spelling and grammar computer-checked to near perfection—in other words, thoroughly professional-looking except on close reading."

I'm sure ewe have scene sum of those samples of computer checked righting that have several errors the spellchecker failed to catch. Eye don't think ewe want that two bee the quality of work ewe produce four the kingdom of God. (Not one of the words used incorrectly in this paragraph, was noted by Microsoft's spellchecker!)

As a writer who is always on guard to catch my own errors, I do have to chuckle when I see a typo in traditionally published books, especially books that are specifically about writing! That just helps me realize that no one is perfect and that when I make a mistake I don't have to beat myself up over it.

Without question, the prospect of someone editing his or her work and possibly finding errors, coupled with the fear of receiving rejection slips from publishers he or she submitted to, are the two greatest hindrances that keep potentially great writers from actually publishing.

Most of the writers I surveyed had trusted friends or relatives help them with editing. You probably know someone that can help you. Give them some guidelines so you understand what their marks mean. Have them circle misspelled words, underline unclear passages, note rough transitions with a question mark and make notes in the margin. You will find a complete set of standard proofreader's marks in your dictionary under "Proofreader's Marks."

Encourage them to be specific. Tom and Marilyn Ross suggest, "Specific, constructive criticism is like surgery; it cuts out the malignancy and spares the rest of the body. Vague criticism is like chemotherapy; it causes the copy's hair to fall out and makes the thing look sicker than it really is."

I would suggest that you not overwhelm one person by sending them the entire document to edit, unless you know that it is not a strain on their time. Have someone edit for you whose advice you can take, not someone that you feel is highly critical of you. And I suggest that you not send it to a person who loves you so much there is no way they could ever criticize anything you wrote! This type of friend can be best helpful by writing a glowing testimonial for you to include on the back cover that will help to sell your book.

Oftentimes, feedback from friends and relatives is unreliable. They may be too accommodating or too critical. Joel Saltzman said, "Praise will stop you from growing, scorn from even trying." You need to have a realistic balance of both to produce your greatest work.

If you choose to have a friend or relative edit for you, make sure you reward them in some way. An offering or honorarium is appropriate, or if you know they will not take money, purchase a nice gift to show your appreciation.

Peer review and editing is a concept that I find helpful. Send out a couple of chapters to experts in your field (friends perhaps who do the same type of work you are writing about) and ask them to review your material for technical details. Ask them to comment in the margins whether it is easy to read, whether you have stated facts correctly, and if what you have written is understandable. Ask them for comments that you can include on the back for testimonials. Peers are good for content editing but you need to find at least two people with the ability to proofread, to carefully check your work. "A good editor challenges you to create your best work," says Pegi Taylor.

As Joel Saltzman said, "Remember, writing is a two-step process. First you find the gold, then you polish it." Editing helps you find the gold.

Again, don't take criticism personally, they are not criticizing you, they are criticizing something you wrote. I have had to refuse to edit for people because I knew that my remarks would be too painful for them. Not because they were a poor writer, but because they had not reached the stage of "elephant's skin"! I admit, it took me a while to get there too, so I understand.

Keep in mind that opinions will vary. One person may think what you wrote is horrible, another person may think it is the best thing that they ever read. Sift through everyone's comments and try to figure out what seems right to you. If several people say the same thing, you'd better listen! One author said, "Everyone gets a vote, but you get to count them!"

Don't allow yourself to feel overwhelmed when you begin polishing your book. Don't be too critical of yourself or become defensive. The attitude "I could do better" rather than "This is no good, therefore I'm no good and who do I think I am trying to write this anyway?" is the way to go. Writing takes work, a lot of work!

Nona Freeman, a former missionary and prolific writer, threw her first manuscript in the trash, as many writers have, only to fish it out, polish it up and resubmit it. It was published and became a best seller at the Pentecostal Publishing House. (Isaac Bashevis Singer said, "A writer's best friend is the wastepaper basket!")

Setting aside your manuscript for a while is a very good editing strategy. When you return to it, you are more objective.

Simplify your writing. Don't be afraid to cut out superfluous words. Keep it simple, direct and to the point.

One of the best pieces of advice I ever read was: write like you talk. How simple and yet how true! When we talk, we talk fluidly, not in long drawn out arduously descriptive paragraphs and sentences. Use simple, everyday language. It doesn't have to be serious, complicated or impressive sounding. Reading your work out loud helps you to hear what sounds like talking and what sounds like writing. Get rid of the gobbledygook!

What author's books do you enjoy most? You probably enjoy those that are easily understood and flow like the author is talking to you personally. That needs to be your goal in writing.

As you "rewrite," don't be afraid to expand in areas where not enough information is given. (Just make sure you have it proofread again!)

Know when to quit! "If you are a perfectionist, you are guaranteed to be a loser in whatever you do," says David Burns, M.D.

"Perfectionism leads to paralysis, which leads to procrastination." (Joel Saltzman) Remember, it doesn't have to be perfect!

At some point you just have to quit editing and get it to print! Accept the fact that there will probably be an error or two in the final product and go on. Nothing and no one is perfect except the Lord Jesus Christ!

Chapter 11

Typesetting and Printing

Typesetting is the process of converting your manuscript into professional, easy-to-read text. It is setting your manuscript up to be printed. In days gone by, it actually meant placing individual letters in trays to be copied, page by page.

You can do your own typesetting, you can pay someone to do it for you, or you can have the book printer do it for you. When you do your own typesetting and send it to the printer, you need to send it "camera-ready." Camera-ready is a term that means it is ready to be shot by their camera without any additional typesetting or alterations. What the camera sees, is what you will see when it is printed. The quality of the printed page you send the book printer will determine the final outcome of your book, therefore, is imperative that your pages be clean and that your print be crisp.

If you choose to have someone else do your typesetting, they will probably require that you send them a typewritten copy of your manuscript to avoid the problems of transposing handwritten copy to type. Make sure you send them a manuscript that is as neat and clean as possible and that you give them clear directions as to what you want in italics, bold face and capitals. They may even ask for your manuscript on a flash drive or on a CD. Typesetting costs approximately $5.00 per page.

Justify your text. Justifying your text makes each line touch the right margin. The left side of type is automatically justified, but without specifying this in your word processor, the right side of the page will look ragged and unprofessional.

As you set up your text, remember to print on only one side of the paper. On your copy (matter you set to type) you must include margin allowances. For a standard book having pages that are 5 ½" x 8 ½," the actual copy, after space is allowed for margins, is 4 3/8" x 7 ½." For an 8 ½ " x 11" book, your actual copy is 7 3/8" x 10." All type must be contained in this area or it will not print. The book printer you choose to go with will give you the standard dimensions they work with according to the size of your finished work. Follow them closely. They will probably have a guide to help you set up your margins to meet their printing needs. You can choose to have your book any size you want, but if you deviate from the standard size, you will pay more money.

Plan how you want your book to look and be consistent throughout. Chapter title pages can have a decorative touch with clip art, or a fancy font. You might want to begin each chapter with a relevant quotation or a scripture. Type your chapter title and leave a couple of blank spaces. Begin your text approximately 1/3 of the way down the page. Traditionally, nonfiction begins on the right-hand side of the page. Fiction is a little more flexible and can begin on either side of the page.

As you plan your margins, leave plenty of white space. Margins are a very important aspect that contributes to the readability of your book. For good visual balance, you should have more room at the bottom of the page than at the top.

Type your manuscript in black ink. If you choose to have your book printed in another color ink they will do it for an additional charge, but most books are printed in black ink.

Most companies will have you center your type on the page and they will trim the excess paper away.

Try to print your camera-ready copy on a laser printer with 300dpi or higher resolution for text pages. It is also good to have a new ink cartridge to assure the darkest print. Ink jet print looks okay to the naked eye, but when it is copied, the print is not clear and crisp. Also, make sure you use laser paper because the toner adheres better and the type prints sharper. Never send dot matrix pages unless you are having them typeset for you.

Page numbers are usually on the bottom of the page approximately ½" up from the bottom. You can have the page number centered, or you can have even page numbers on the left hand side of the page and odd page number on the right-hand side of the page. You don't have to put numbers on blank pages, but they do count in your number of pages and the printer needs to know you have left pages blank for a reason.

You want your type to look professional. Look at books you have read to get an idea of what looks good. The font you choose will determine the readability of your book. Self-publishers like to experiment with different types and styles of fonts. Script fonts are difficult to read and do not invite eyes to read them. Choose a type that is easy on the eyes.

There are two basic kinds of fonts: serif type and sans serif. Serifs are the short cross-lines at the ends of the main strokes of letters. They are the finishing touches on letters, especially capital letters. They act as little hooks that grab the eye's attention. Sans serif type is difficult to read because it does not have the little "hooks."

Text font is usually 10, 11, 12, or 14-point size. Keep in mind that fonts with the same point size are not necessarily the same size in print. For example: Palatino is a larger style font and will produce less words per page than say Times New Roman. (Morris Press has a wonderful publishing guide that compares typeset done in different fonts to give you an idea of what they will look like. This can be ordered for free from their web-site, by mail, or by phone. This information is in the reference sections.)

Chapter headings can be a different font than you are using for your text and are typed in a larger font size. They are usually set in bold type and are sometimes italicized. As you type, use boldface or italics, not underlines, to add emphasis.

You will need to find a book printer. Some authors use the same book printer for all of their books, others look around to see who can best meet their time constraints or who can save them money. Several names are mentioned in the survey and I will address each of those mentioned, in the appendix. I cannot guarantee any of their work, I am only offering the information as provided to me from authors and sharing with you what has worked for me.

Many of the book printers can be found on the internet with complete guidelines at your fingertips. If you prefer to have a hard copy, you can write or call them and they will be happy to accommodate you.

Self-Publishing has dramatically changed in the last ten years. No longer do you need to send print copies to them. Most often they have a website that you will be able to upload your files to.

They will be happy to do your editing and typesetting for you but you could incur major expenses. You would be safer to have an editor help you to get as much as you can get completed before you begin your upload, including your cover.

There are several Print On Demand, or POD's that are available today. Print on demand (POD) book publishing is when copies of a book are not printed until an order is placed for that book. For self publishing authors, print on demand book publishing services make it convenient to sell physical copies of their books without having to pay an enormous upfront costs for bulk printing storage.

The print on demand publishing company usually offers their service for a fee. Services normally include printing, shipping to the customers, handling royalties, and often listing the books in online bookstores, such as Amazon. Some companies also offer services such as formatting, proofreading, and editing.

Print on demand publishing gives authors editorial independence, speedy marketability, ability to revise their content at will, and typically a greater return per book than profits made with traditional publishers.

Print on demand (POD) book publishing is when copies of a book are not printed until an order is placed for that book. For self publishing authors, print on demand book publishing services make it convenient to sell physical copies of their books without having to pay an enormous upfront cost for bulk printing.

Morris Publishing is where I had my first two books printed. They were very easy to work with, did a top-notch job, met all of my deadlines and did not charge me a penny more than we agreed upon. I really felt they had my best interest at heart and helped me produce a book that rivals major publishers. The Pentecostal Publishing House did my third book. My latest book was done with Create Space. I was very pleased with the results.

Whatever printer you choose to go with is up to you, but I would certainly want references from any company prior to committing my project to them.

More than likely, the printer will send you a proof of your text pages to allow you to check to see that everything is the way you want it to be, before it is printed. Check it carefully. If they have made a mistake in the setup, they will make the corrections without a charge to you. If you find typos that need corrected, you will have to pay a per page fee to make those changes and if it entails a situation that changes page numbers it could be very costly. (I almost think it's best not to look! Just kidding!)

Keep your timeline in check. If you have a particular date that you are planning to have your book finished by, perhaps a speaking engagement or a book signing, you need to allow plenty of time for unforeseen circumstances. Problems can arise and rush orders cost more!

I've been told that book printers are not very busy at the beginning of the year so it is a good time to contact them. They begin to get busy in the early spring. Holidays extend printing time, so try to avoid them.

Another important thing to consider is how many books you plan to have printed. The more books you have printed, the less each book will cost you. Most of the cost in printing involves the set up fees. Preparing the negatives and plates and setting up the presses takes just as much time to prepare to print 500 copies as it does to print 20,000. Be realistic in your estimate of how many books you will sell. Major book publishers often only print 6,000 copies until they see how it will do on the market. I would suggest printing around 1,000 copies, especially if you are a new author, unless you are sure you will sell more. You can always get more printed and it will cost less because they already have your book ready to go. (This is where the concept of P.O.D., Print on Demand, would come in handy, if you are sure it is a reputable company.)

If you are a fairly well known speaker or you have other books out that have sold well, you would be safe having more books printed.

Printing costs vary according to the printer you choose. The size of your book, the type of binding you choose and the cover will all be factors in the cost of manufacturing.

Shipping is also a cost factor to consider. They will probably give you the option to have all the books sent to one address or to have books sent to various addresses. Sending them to more than one address will probably result in additional costs, plus you must make sure that the recipient is aware of the shipment and that he or she is willing to check that they arrive in good condition and that the correct number was received. I have found it easier to have all the books shipped to my home for storage. When books are ordered, I pass along the shipping charges to the buyer, as do most businesses.

Most printers will work out a payment arrangement with you. They may require a certain percentage when you place your order, another percent when you receive your proof, and the balance, with shipping charges, when your books are sent to you. They will probably accept payment by credit card as well as check or money order. It's always better if you have the cash to pay for your books rather than presume on the future and charge your order.

You will need to determine how much your book will be sold for. This information will need to be given to the company that designs your bar code, because it is imbedded in the code. You want to price the book so that it pays for itself and to allow for discounts as you sell them. There will also be copies that are given away for advertising and reviewing and you need to cover them in your expenses. The best thing to do is find a book on the market that is similar in size and price your book accordingly. There is a trick to numbers and how they affect our purchases. Nines always seem to sell better than zeros! $10.95 and $10.99 just seem more appealing than $11.00 for some reason. Again, take your cue from a book that is currently on the market.

The exact number of books you order is rarely what you receive. In printing, due to spoilage, printers have an "overrun/underrun policy" that states that you could receive up to 10% more books than you ordered or up to 10% less books than you ordered! More than likely, you will receive an overrun and you need to budget for the additional cost of the books and their shipping.

Chapter 12

Last Minute Checks

When your manuscript is ready, contact the printer you have decided to go with. Discuss with them the procedure you need to follow to get your manuscript to them. They will probably assign you a number for your print order and a person that you will work with. It would be nice to have the luxury of visiting the printing company in person and sitting down with their representative. Few authors have this opportunity unless they go with a locally owned printer as Crawford Coon did. He felt it was much more personal and that he could move quickly with changes.

If you have requested their publishing guide, there is probably a form to fill out and a guide to help you figure the cost of printing your book. If you do not have this information, perhaps their website will have it.

The printer will want to know the size of your book, the weight of paper you want it to be printed on, the color of ink, the type of cover you want and how it will be bound. They will also want to know who will be responsible for designing your cover. They will want to know how you are planning to pay for it. They do accept charge cards.

As you search for a printing company, compare prices, but don't automatically go with the cheapest one. There may be a reason why they are cheaper. Some Print on Demand companies are said to use toner rather than ink and it may not hold up as well on paper. Look at samples of their books. If you don't have a sample, ask for one.

Look for a full-service book manufacturer who specializes in books. Their prices are more reasonable, they know the ins and outs of the business and they do everything in house.

I have found it best to talk to people who have self-published to get their feedback on companies they have worked with, and to look at the quality of their books.

From the survey I took, two companies were mentioned over and over. They were praised for their professionalism, quality of work, reliability and ease of working with as well as their reasonable prices.

Morris Publishing was mentioned most frequently. Authors such as Daniel L. Segraves, Judy Segraves, LaJoyce Martin, Ruth Rieder, Roffie Ensey, Gayla Baughman, and Lynda Allison Doty, Arlo Moehlenpall and Thomas Weisser have used their services and been very satisfied.

Moeller Printing was also mentioned several times. Arlo Moehlenpall choose Moeller Printing for one of his books because he felt they were the only company that could produce the quality of pictures he needed and they were willing to work with him on a rush order. J.T. Pugh and Marvelle Dees also had Moeller print their books and have been very happy with them.

Several authors mentioned they have used various printers according to their particular needs.

Jim H. Yohe shared the following, "After several companies I discovered Genesis Communications in Mobile, Alabama. I have done several books with him, Brian Banashak. He is an outstanding cover designer, and he is a print broker. He takes your book's specifics and puts them into an international publisher's chatroom and obtains bids from all over the world. You get a very good price delivered to your door as well as an eye-catching cover that will increase your sales. I've been advised to try Moeller Printing in Indianapolis by several authors. If they bother to bid, I've always found them to be $900-$1500 higher."

Missionary Nona Freeman has always used Faith Publishing. She has developed a very close working relationship with them and visits their company when she can. She likes their terms and services.

Shirley Englehardt actually prints her own books and binds them with a plastic comb-binding machine. She controls literally every aspect of her books.

Whatever company you choose, get your agreement in writing and insist on seeing proofs, even if you have to pay a little more for them.

Proof the cover very carefully. Check the spelling the wording and the colors. In *Growing in All the Right Places*, the cover had a dark spot where the color looked muddied. They were able to brighten it up and it came out beautiful. Remember, your cover is your main advertisement.

Check for errors in pagination, margins, headings, the placement of illustrations and photos and the position of the text on the page. Check to see if the bar code is correct. Are the pages crooked? Are there light spots or blurry type? Double check to see that the ISBN number is correct.

You may be able to get an overrun on your cover that you can use for advertising your book. You can have the table of contents and ordering information printed on the back of the cover. This can be used as a mail out to solicit orders. You can also have bookmarks printed and probably posters done as well, but keep the costs in mind!

They will need to know how you want your books shipped and where they are to be delivered. Depending on the number of books, they may come by UPS® as mine did, or they may deliver them on pallets from a semi. When they arrive, check to see if the number of boxes and the number of books all add up. They will probably have the boxes numbered and indicate how many books are in each box. You also want to check to see if there has been any damage. If there is damage, you will need to file a report for the shipper to make restitution for damaged copies.

Chapter 13

Is Self-Publishing A Business?

Self-publishing is a business and needs to be treated as such. You will have tax liabilities but you will also have tax deductions associated with your business. You need to keep very good records detailing all expenses related to your business.

Anyone can be a publisher. The "publisher" of a book is the one who puts up the money, the one who takes the risk, the investor. To be a publisher, you do not need a license or to register with any agency, but most publishers do register their books with the International Standard Book Numbers (ISBN), the Library of Congress and the United States Copyright Office.

If you sell books in your home state, you are liable for the taxes. You need to have a business ID number from your state.

If you want to sell your book on a broader scale than just what you yourself can sell, it is wise to have your book registered with the three agencies mentioned above. Your book can be traced for purchase from any place in the world if it has an ISBN number. The ISBN number traces the book to the publisher. If someone wanted your book they could look up the number and receive information needed to contact you, the publisher, to purchase your book.

ISBN numbers are available to purchase through Browkers. In the past an author/publisher was able to purchase one number for approximately $50.00 but that option is no longer available. Now you must purchase the numbers in lots of 10 for approximately $250.00.

When I originally contacted my book printer, they were willing to act as the publisher. However, by the time my book was ready to be printed, they had changed their policy. Because they have no rights to your book and they do not warehouse it, they would have to forward all inquiries to the author. This became too cumbersome for them so they dropped the policy.

Marketing

Sales of any book, self-published or not, basically come down to promotion by the author. As Christians it often seems uncomfortable promoting yourself, but when you know you have a product that can help people in their spiritual development and their walk with God, you need not be ashamed to do so. Your excitement will increase sales as will the excitement of those you have helped via your writing or speaking. Word of mouth is a powerful tool. If people know you and trust you, they will tell others and they will buy your book.

You need to develop a plan as to how you will sell your books in bulk. I have sold most of my books through our denomination's publishing house. As the distributor, I sell books to them a discount and they pay the shipping charges to get the books to them. Churches or small bookstores may ask you to sell to them with a discount. I sell up to ten books with a 10% discount. Over ten books, I give the standard discount of 30%. You need to set up a sales plan and be consistent with your prices. If one person or group finds out you have sold your products to other people for less than they paid, you will loose your credibility with them. You will not make as much money on the books you sell in bulk, but you will sell more.

You will probably have the opportunity to have the company who is printing your book, also print posters, bookmarks, or postcards, which can be used as advertising tools.

Identify and target your audience. How can you reach them? What catalogs might be interested? Which associations reach your potential readers?

Check with your denomination's headquarters to see if they have a website or catalog that could be used to advertise your book. If you have an article published in a magazine or newspaper, make sure you mention your book and how perspective buyers can contact you. You can send postcards advertising your books to potential buyers that may be unaware of its publication.

If you live in a relatively small community, your local newspaper may be interested in writing a feature article about you and your book. They will interview you in person or over the phone and probably print a picture with the article. It will lead to local exposure, help you sell some books, possibly open up speaking engagements, as it did for me, and perhaps be a venue to share your testimony.

If you are really aggressive and want more coverage and opportunities, you might consider contacting Christian radio stations or Public Broadcasting stations to see if they would be interested in interviewing you on a program. They say this avenue is more available than we think it is.

Entire books have been written to help self-publishers market their products. If your goal is to tap into a large market, I would suggest you read one of the many books that are available to determine the most effective path to take.

Appendix

The Process of Self-Publishing

1.   Develop the idea.
2.   The book itself may take years of writing.
3.   Research.
4.   Get a model book.
5.   Decide on a working title.
6.   Develop the inside pages:
        Prepare the manuscript.
        Develop style sheet to follow.
        Write the front and back material.
7.   Design cover:
        Color scheme, graphic design or picture, font: color, size.
        Write cover front and back matter.
8.   Develop book style:
     Decide on the size of the finished book.
     Decide on the type of binding:
        Hardback
        Perfect Binding (most popular)
        3-Ring Binding
        Plastic Coil
        Plastic Comb
9.   Set up your binder with dividers, and put a mock-up of your cover in the pockets.
10. Assemble research materials in proper chapters.
11. Write first draft.
12. Peer review your material.
13. Decide how you will publish:
        Sell to publisher or Self-Publish
14. Register book for copyright.
15. Obtain ISBN number.
16. Choose book printer.
17. Contact book printers to get estimates on printing costs.
18. Finish typesetting

19. Edit
20. Package and send manuscript to book printer. Package carefully and send in a box if possible so pages will remain neat.

Resources

Editor, highly recommended by Christian self-published authors:

Bethany Sledge
cnbsledge@gmail.com

Printing companies highly recommended by Christian self-published authors:

Morris Publishing
Morrispublishing.com
3212 E. Hwy 30
Kearney, NE 68847
1-800-650-7888

Pentecostal Publishing House
36 Research Park Ct.
Weldon Springs, MO63304

Word Aflame House Rules*
(Pentecostal Publishing House)

1. All Bible verses used in Word Aflame (Scripture Lesson, Bible verses, etc.) are taken from the King James Version. We also use the Cambridge Bible as our guide for punctuation, capitalization, etc.

   However, if in the lesson the writer refers to another translation, it should be noted. But the King James Version should still be used as the primary Scripture source.

   EXAMPLE; "And he ordered that they be baptized in the name of Jesus Christ, the Messiah" (Acts 10:48, *The Amplified Bible*).

2. Quote verses of Scripture word for word, dot for dot, comma for comma! DOUBLE-CHECK ALL SCRIPTURES WITH THE BIBLE for spelling, punctuation, and reference.

3. DO NOT abbreviate the books of the Bible. (Revelation 1:2, NOT Rev. 1:2)

4. When listing verses of Scripture, separate them with a semicolon. (Leviticus 19:11; Romans 6:23; Acts 2:38; John 3:16)

5. Use Roman numerals, not Arabic, in reference to books of the Bible. (II Corinthians 9:16, NOT 2 Corinthians 9:16)

6. When quoting a portion of a verse of Scripture, use ellipses following this style:

   a. Beginning—"For we shall see him."
      (NOT "…for we shall see him.")

      And we shall all "see him as he is."
      (NOT And we shall all "…see him as he is."

b. Middle—"Beloved…we shall see him."

c. End—"Beloved, now we are…."

(If the ellipsis ends the sentence, use four dots; if not, use three as in the other examples.)

d. End—"Beloved, now are we …" (I John 3:2)

(If a Scripture reference follows the ellipsis, use three dots following the quotation and a period following the reference.)

The use of ellipsis is not particularly necessary if only one word at the beginning of a verse, such as a conjunction, is omitted. Also, if the portion of Scripture used contains a complete thought, the ellipses are not necessary at the beginning or end. In the first example above, since the words quoted form a sentence when the words "as he is" are omitted, there is no need for the ellipsis. Also if a verse of Scripture contains two complete sentences and only one is to be used, the ellipsis is not necessary. Always use the ellipsis, however, if a portion of Scripture is omitted from the middle of a passage.

7. Use the past tense when possible in reference to bible times. (Paul stated. NOT Paul states)

8. References to a particular Psalm and to the Book of Revelation should be indicated with the singular form of the word. (Psalm 44:9, NOT Psalms 44:9. Revelation 3:4, NOT Revelations 3:4. However, it is correct to write the Book of Psalms.)

9. Capitalize He, Him, His, Thine, You, Your when referring to God, but do not capitalize them when used in quoting verses of Scripture if they are not capitalized in the Bible.

10. The following is a list of typical terms used in the Word Aflame offices:
    Con-Tact paper   Kool-Aid (Brand name, capitalized)
    Plaster of Paris   Play-Doh (Brand name, capitalized)
    Papier-mache   Plasti-Tak (Brand name, capitalized)

11. Single quotation marks are used to set off a quotation within a quotation.

EXAMPLE: Mary whispered, "Did she say, 'I'll never return'?"

12. To quote from copyrighted sources, the author must obtain written permission from the owner of the copyright, usually the publisher. When writing for permission to quote, mention the author, title, editor, page number, and the amount of quotation, noting what words the quotation begins with. The letters of permission are to be turned over to Word Aflame Publications for filing. It is a common practice among most publishers to quote a maximum of 50 consecutive words (or in the case of songs and poetry, two lines) from a copyrighted source without obtaining permission. Material published before 1906 may be quoted freely without permission as it belongs to public domain. To pick up another's work, whether copyrighted or not, and pawn it off as one's own is unethical in any case.

13. Headings or titles may be either all capitals or capital and lowercase. (In this case, capitalize only the principle words; lowercase "a," "the," or prepositions and conjunctions.)

14. A period or comma is always placed inside closing quotation marks.

EXAMPLE: He mispronounced the word "epistle."
"I will come again," he said.

15. A question mark or exclamation point is placed inside the quotation marks when it belongs to the quoted matter. It is placed outside the quotation marks when it belongs to the whole sentence or clause including the question.

EXAMPLE: He asked, "Will you be ready?"
Did he say, "You will be ready"?

16. A colon or semicolon is placed outside closing quotation marks unless they are part of the quoted matter.

EXAMPLE: He said, "Be ye also ready"; therefore, I am preparing.

17. In typewritten manuscript, use a double hyphen, unspaced before and after, to represent an em dash.

EXAMPLE: His mind was like concrete-thoroughly mixed up
                      And permanently set.

18. Enclose a direct quote of the Scriptures in quotation marks. Follow the verse with the place it is found in the Bible in parentheses. The period should follow the closing parenthesis.

    EXAMPLE: "Jesus wept" (John 11:35).
                      NOT "Jesus wept." (John 11:35)

    When the verse of Scripture is a question, the question mark is placed before the last quotation marks, and the period follows the parenthesis.

    EXAMPLE: "Saul, Saul, why persecutest thou me?" (Acts 9:4).

19. A reference to the verse of Scripture, but not the direct quote, should be punctuated in the same manner as the reference.

    EXAMPLE: "As a man, Jesus felt grief and wept (John 11:35).
                      NOT As a man, Jesus felt grief and wept. (John 11:35)

20. If directing readers to certain references, follow this method:

    EXAMPLE: Persons receiving the Holy Ghost will speak with
                      Tongues. (See Acts 2:4; 10:46.)

Spelling and Capitalization

Words frequently misspelled:

Correct Spelling	Incorrect Spelling *
anointed	NOT annointed
any more	NOT anymore
apostasy	NOT apostacy
baptistery	NOT baptistry
cannot	NOT can not
commitment	NOT committment
committed	NOT commited
committee	NOT commitee
everyone	NOT every one
everywhere	NOT every where
fence	NOT fense
judgment	NOT judgement
lifestyle	NOT life-style or life style
lightning	NOT lifntening
loneliness	NOT lonliness
offense	NOT offence
precede	NOT preceed or preseed
prophecy	
"that which is uttered:	(e.g. The prophecy was given.)
prophesy	
"the act of uttering"	(e.g. the prophet will prophesy.)
reinforce	NOT reinforse
resurrection	NOT ressurection
Savior	NOT Saviour (except in Scripture quotations)
steadfast	NOT stedfast (except in Scripture quotations)
supersede	NOT supercede or superceed
threshold	NOT threshhold
traveled	NOT travelled (except in Scripture

quotations)

Worshiped	NOT worshipped (except in Scripture Quotations.
Worshiping	NOT worshipping (except in Scripture quotations)

* Some of these spellings are not wrong, but they are not preferred.

*These last five pages were used with permission from J. L. Hall, former Chairman of Word Aflame Press. They were taken directly from the Word Aflame House Rules packet, a guideline for authors submitting work to their publication. They represent the desired style unique to Christian writing and publication. They constitute an intensely beneficial reference.

Glossary of Self-Publishing Terms

Bar code- gives the book identification and price, usually found on back covers of books and read by computer scanners at checkout counters

Bluelines- printer's proofs designed to catch final errors before printing

Book bindings:
Hard bound- hardcover
Comb- spiral-like plastic binding used when authors want books to lie flat
Perfect- a square spine created by gluing the page ends together at the spine
Saddle-stitch- stapled at the fold, like a magazine, usually used for small books
Spiral- wire binding often used on notebooks

Copyright- authors' and artists' right to license and control publication of the work they create

Camera-ready copy- text and artwork completely ready for the printer

Direct mail- advertising mailed directly to potential customers

Editing- making changes in a manuscript

Endorsements- flattering remarks about a book, usually found on the back cover

Foreword- beginning remarks in a book about the book and its author

ISBN- International Standard Book Number, essential to the identification of a particular book

Permissions- permission to use text or art from another copyrighted work

POD- Print on Demand- the process of printing books only when they are ordered

Print runs:

Overrun- the number of copies in excess of the number requested that are printed at the same time as the initial print run

Underrun- the number of copies under the number requested in the printing contract

Review copies- books given away to those who write book reviews

Short run- designation given to small print runs, usually just a few hundred books

Signatures- the page multiples in which books are most often printed: 4,8,12,16,32

Bibliography

The Writer's Digest Guide to Manuscript Formats, (Writer's Digest Books), by Dian Dincin Buchman and Seli Groves.

How to Write and Sell Your Personal Experiences, by Lois Duncan.

Writing Articles From the Heart (Writer's Digest Books), by Marjorie Holmes.

101 Ways to Market Your Books, John Kremer.

Is There a Book Inside You, (Para Publishing), by Dan Poynter.

The Self-Publishing-Manual: How to Write, Print, and Sell Your Own Book (Para Publishing), by Dan Poynter.

The Complete Guide to Self-Publishing (Writer's Digest Books), 3d ed., by Marilyn and Tom Ross.

If You Can Talk, You Can Write, Saltzman, Joel, Warner Books, NY 1993.

The Elements of Style, William Strunk and E. B. White.

How to Write the Story of Your Life, (Writer's Digest Books), by Frank P. Thomas.

Christian Writers' Market Guide, Sally E. Stuart. (Each year she produces a new volume with the current information.)

The Writer's Market, Writer's Digest Books.

Guerrilla Marketing For Writers, Jay Conrad Levinson, Rick Frishman, and Michael Larson. (An aggressive approach to marketing your book.)

Notes: